Tetsuyo Ishii was born in 1920 in Jogecho, Hiroshima. She worked as an elementary school teacher from age twenty to fifty-six, before working full-time on her family's allotment. Locals still affectionately call her 'Teacher'. She was featured in the *Chugoku Shimbun* newspaper and on TV, where her vitality and personality rocketed her to national fame.

Happy on Her Own at 102

With thanks to Naomi Suzunaka,
Yoko Kinomoto and Takahiro Inoue for
providing the photographs.

Happy on Her Own at 102

A guide to living a long
and happy life

TETSUYO ISHII
with THE CHUGOKU SHIMBUN

Translated by Arthur Reiji Morris

LEAP

First published in the UK in 2026 by LEAP
An imprint of Bonnier Books UK
5th Floor, HYLO, 105 Bunhill Row,
London, EC1Y 8LZ

102-SAI HITORIGURASHI. Tetsuyo Obaachan no Kokoro mo Karada mo Sabinai
Ikikata by ISHII Tetsuyo, The Chugoku Shimbun.
Copyright © ISHII Tetsuyo, The Chugoku Shimbun 2023
All rights reserved.

Original Japanese edition published by Bungeishunju Ltd. in 2023.
English translation rights in PRC reserved by Bonnier Books UK Limited under the
licence granted by ISHII Tetsuyo and The Chugoku Shimbun, Japan, arranged with
Bungeishunju Ltd., Japan, through Curtis Brown Group Ltd., UK.
English translation copyright © Arthur Reiji Morris
All rights reserved.

No part of this publication may be reproduced, stored or transmitted in
any form or by any means, electronic, mechanical, photocopying or otherwise, without
the prior written permission of the publisher.

The right of Tetsuyo Ishii and The Chugoku Shimbun to be identified as
Author of this work has been asserted by them in accordance with the Copyright,
Designs and Patents Act, 1988.

A CIP catalogue record for this book is available from the British Library.

Hardback ISBN: 9781806170081

Also available as an ebook and an audiobook

1 3 5 7 9 10 8 6 4 2

Design and Typeset by Envy Design Ltd
Printed and bound by CPI (UK) Ltd, Croydon CR0 4YY

Every reasonable effort has been made to trace copyright holders of
material reproduced in this book, but if any have been inadvertently
overlooked the publishers would be glad to hear from them.

The authorised representative in the EEA is
Bonnier Books UK (Ireland) Limited.
Registered office address: Block B, The Crescent Building
Northwood, Santry
Dublin 9, D09 C6X8, Ireland
compliance@bonnierbooks.ie

www.bonnierbooks.co.uk

Contents

To Begin: 'Become a pro at encouraging
yourself and cheering up your own heart'   1
A Note from the translator   5
An Introduction to Granny Tetsuyo   7
Granny Tetsuyo's Eight Habits for Living
a Long and Healthy Life   13

**Chapter 1: From Age 100 to 101: 'Today's
a good day.'**   21

    Granny Tetsuyo's Diary at Age 100
        October 2020: Be like a hoe that
        never rusts   22

November 2020: Instead of complaining, try and stay busy	29
December 2020: A life without hard work is a boring life	37
February 2021: Working for the joys to come	45
March 2021: How I reached one hundred years old	51
April 2021: Find joy in repetition	59
May 2021: Your mood depends on yourself	67
Granny Tetsuyo's Diary at Age 101	73
June 2021: Cherishing days spent alone October 2021: Learning to let go	77
November 2021: Spending the end of my life in a cheerful and charming way	81
December 2021: Chatting about the good times with friends	89

Chapter 2: Tell Us More About Yourself, Granny Tetsuyo!   95

Chapter 3: Grateful for Life at 102   113
  Correspondence from Granny Tetsuyo
    February 2022: Hospitalised due to
    her weight?   114
    March 2022: I'd like to keep on living
    here, day by day   116
    April 2022: The secret to ageing well   121
    June 2022: The five principles for being
    true to myself   125

**Chapter 4: Granny Tetsuyo's Tasty Recipes
for a Long Life**   133

A Closing Message from the Paper   141
Aspirations for 2023   147

*Eat in abundance, sleep in abundance,
chat in abundance.*

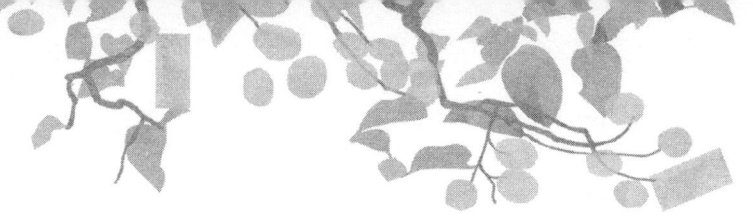

To Begin: 'Become a pro at encouraging yourself and cheering up your own heart.'

Ahh, now that's nice. I've just woken up from a nap. I was hard at work in the field all morning so I had a little doze after lunch. Such is life on your own. You don't need to worry about troubling anyone else and you're free and easy. People often ask if I have trouble falling asleep at night, but don't you worry about that. As soon as I tuck myself in, I'm out like a light, snoring away.

Right, now that I'm properly awake, I should introduce myself. My name is Tetsuyo Ishii, I am 102 years old. When I was a little girl, I thought that a

Happy on Her Own at 102

one-hundred-year-old lady was someone who only appeared in fairy tales, but here I find myself past that landmark. It's quite the surprise.

I live in a town between the mountains in Onomichi, Hiroshima. I moved here when I got married at twenty-six years old. I worked as a teacher until I was fifty-six, working in our rice paddies all the while. I wasn't blessed with any children and have been living on my own since my husband passed away twenty years ago. My days are filled with taking care of a small field and chatting to my neighbours.

My quiet everyday life got a little bit more lively soon after I turned 100. My local paper, the *Chugoku Shimbun*, did a serialised feature about my daily life. It was filled with all sorts of my silly nonsense like, 'We got a good crop of daikon radishes this year', or, 'I had three mochi rice cakes in my ozoni soup this New Year.' To my surprise I received a lot of letters from people telling me their thoughts or giving their own encouragement. I was truly overjoyed.

Then, to add surprise to surprise, they told me they were going to publish it as a book! Wow, how incredible. I felt myself rising to heaven then coming

Tetsuyo Ishii

back down again. I was happy enough just living well at this age, so this truly took me aback.

As you get older, there are ever more things that you can't do, and there are days when your heart completely shuts off from everybody. But complaints don't solve a thing. I want to become a pro at encouraging myself and cheering up my heart. You can't change people, but you can change aspects about yourself, after all. This book is full of little titbits like that from this old lady. I'm sure my husband is reading this book with a big smile from the afterlife.

A Note from the Translator

BY ARTHUR REIJI MORRIS

With its famously high life expectancy, people across the globe look to Japan for tips on how to live longer, looking for the diet or lifestyle secret to unlock more time on Earth. Indeed, the ultra-rich in particular seem to be exploring ways to live forever at any cost. It goes without saying that they won't find what they are looking for here.

Granny Tetsuyo became a target of adoration for many people when the *Chugoku Shimbun*, her local newspaper, featured her in print and on TV. I believe that the reason why Tetsuyo stole the hearts of so many wasn't due to any sort of arcane secrets she might

Happy on Her Own at 102

harbour as to her long life (although she does give her own share of tips about how she approaches life). No, her appeal is her charming mix of realism and zest for life. Tetsuyo embraces ageing. As she tends to her little field throughout the seasons, she is constantly aware of her limits and how her body changes with each passing year. She accepts when something no longer is possible; she accepts each changing stage of her life. For many young people, in Japan and across the world too, everyday life can be such an uphill struggle that it's easy to lose sight of the small things. Tetsuyo's simple life is a salve. To hear her finding the small joys in a cherry blossom viewing or a larger crop of potatoes isn't a longevity lecture but rather a reminder to everyone that the joy of long life comes from living it.

Translating Tetsuyo was an absolute joy. As I read the original text, it felt like I was right there with Tetsuyo and I tried to capture this warm and casual tone, as if she were chatting with you too, over a pot of tea. I hope that readers in English will enjoy their time with Tetsuyo as much as I did.

An Introduction to Granny Tetsuyo

When and where were you born?

I was born in a place called Jogecho. It was a town that is now in Fuchu, Hiroshima. I was born in 1920. That makes me five years older than Suzu from the animated film, *In this Corner of the World*.

What was your job?

I worked as a primary school teacher from the age of twenty to fifty-six, After that, I worked full-time in the fields. People in the neighbourhood still call me 'Sensei'.

Happy on Her Own at 102

Do you have family?
When I was twenty-six I married my husband, Yoshihide, who was also a teacher at the school I worked at, and moved to Minogocho in Onomichi. We never had children and ever since he passed away when I was eighty-three, I've been living on my own. My nieces, neighbours and students often come and visit.

What's your height and weight?
I'm 150cm (although probably a bit smaller now) and weigh 45kg.

What shoe size are you?
Size 3.

What's your favourite food?
I love anything with meat in it. Or any ramen. I can't choose a favourite! If I started to list my favourites in order, I would feel bad for the dishes. After all, I grew up in an age when there wasn't much food to go around.

Tetsuyo Ishii

What's your favourite drink?
Hot Japanese tea.

What kind of house do you live in?
I think the photograph [above] illustrates it well.
I live in a traditional two-storey Japanese house atop a big hill. The kitchen is old with a sunken floor, but I often chat with my neighbours there. We have three rice paddies, but they're a lot of work for one person, so I now leave the rice growing to a friend. I'm happy with tending to my veggies in a little plot.

Do you take care of animals?
I took care of four hens until about two or three years ago. They all had the same name: Kokko-chan. They blessed me with eggs every morning, but they all passed away one day when a weasel got at the poor dears. It made me terribly sad, so I decided not to get any others.

Do you have any siblings?
I'm the second oldest of four siblings. My brothers Taketo and Satoshi have left this world, but my little sister Momoyo is ninety-five and lives in Kobe.

Do you drive?
I have a red mobility scooter made by Suzuki. I bought it when I was eighty-nine and have been using it since.

Do you have any particular skills?
Eating and chatting. I'm particularly good at pulling up weeds.

Do you have a personal motto?
Be like a hoe that never rusts.

Tetsuyo Ishii

What do you grow in your field?
I'm always tending to some sort of crop throughout the year. I gave them a quick count and there's about twenty-one varieties. I also grow flowers to be given at family Buddhist altars or placed on gravestones.

*All ages in the text are from the time of the interview.

Granny Tetsuyo's Eight Habits for Living a Long and Healthy Life

I have a few habits that help me to live comfortably. Refusing to skimp on any of these – doing them properly day in and day out while also enjoying them – has helped me live as long as I have. I would like to share these eight habits with you all.

1. Folding my bedding every day
I generally wake up around 6.30. I used to sleep on a futon on the floor, but ever since the summer of 2020, I have been sleeping on a hospital bed lent out to me. A futon and a bed aren't quite the same, but after

waking up every day, I make sure to fold up my duvet and store it in the futon closet as I always have. This is my first job of the day. I am always reminded what a blessing it is to be able to wake up and be able to fold up your own bedding.

During the colder months, I use three blankets on top of my duvet. My feather duvet is light and warm, but it is quite thick. To avoid dealing with unwieldy bedding, I layer my blankets instead. Even an old lady like me can carry them about with ease! Of course, I don't move them all in one trip – I make two or three journeys. Who needs the gym when you've got all this bedding? It's a daily activity, but I think of it as a form of exercise.

2. Enjoying miso soup with iriko sardines
Ever since I got married at twenty-six, I have made miso soup every single morning. I use iriko sardines in the broth. They don't require too much preparation, you can just throw them in. They're a real anywhere ingredient – you can cut them up and add them to a leafy vegetables and aubergine stir-fry, or you can

boil them with some daikon radish. I think the only animal-based ingredient I have at home is this fish. It truly is my lifeline. Miso soup, rice and some pickles make up my go-to breakfast.

3. Savouring every bite

I've never been a picky eater, even as a child. I also make sure to eat enough. I usually have three meals per day, often featuring a vegetable stir-fry. I just grab what I need from the fields and start chopping. I usually cook two portions of rice for dinner. If I'm making bara-zushi, then I usually load up my plate! I want to make sure I am always grateful for the food I eat, so even when I'm on my own I make sure to say 'Itadakimasu' ['I humbly receive'] before eating, and 'Gochiso-sama' ['That was a feast'] after I've eaten. At around 3 p.m. I'll have some hot tea and a little snack and I always say to myself out loud, 'All right, time for a little snack.' I don't know why, but it always makes me look forward to it.

Today I tried a hamburger for the first time. What a treat! I wonder if it's the mole above my lip that

Happy on Her Own at 102

makes every meal I eat so delicious even at this age? In Japan, they say that the position of a mole near your mouth can affect your fortune. Ever since I was a little girl, I was told that mine was a 'soothing mole' and that I would never trouble for food. It's a little treasure of mine.

4. When the weather is nice, diligently pulling up weeds
On days with nice weather, you can usually find me pulling up the weeds around my house and in the field. It feels like I'm mistreating both my home and the field if they're overrun by weeds.

My mother-in-law would always go and pull up

weeds when she had a spare moment. She would even go so far as pulling up the ones from the street or on the stone walls. Maybe because she was such a good and constant example, I found myself unable to just let them be either. I feel nice and refreshed when I've finished cleaning them up.

Up until about four or five years ago, on New Year's Day, I would always head to the field with my scythe in hand to begin the work for the year. I would always give my greeting for the year: 'Dear hoe, dear field – I look forward to working with you again this year.' I haven't been able to do this recently, though – it's awfully cold!

5. Returning food waste to the earth

I gather my tangerine peels and other inedible vegetable parts in a bag and make compost. My mother-in-law taught me once: 'Feed your field with everything that isn't stone or metal.' I have followed her advice ever since.

I return everything to the earth that can be returned. I have a compost bag in my garden too and

I make sure to collect up all of the weeds I've pulled as well as any fallen leaves. I probably collect sixty bags over the course of the year, then, once the rice has been harvested, I fertilise the paddy with it. This also has the extra benefit of greatly reducing how much waste I make.

6. Training my brain

I've been doing the vocabulary writing practice that comes with the brain training flyers folded into the newspaper where you have to write the correct kanji for each of the words. I like to challenge myself even when I've solved them once, so I make sure to write my answers on a separate piece of paper. I have been getting perfect scores of late. That reminds me – time to solve today's.

7. Saying hello to Yoshihide

My husband Yoshihide-san passed away twenty years ago and I keep a photo of him by my pillow. I open one of the drawers of my bedside cabinet and position the photo there so that I can see his face from the bed. It's strange, but I feel like I can feel his gaze. I'm sure when I do, he's saying, 'You did great today.'

Before I go to sleep, I always say goodnight to him. It makes me feel like he's there with me and that encourages me. Every morning and every evening I pour a cup of his favourite sake and place it at the Buddhist altar. After it has been accepted, I finish the cup myself. He had good taste in drinks.

8. Stretching
Whenever I remember, I make sure to stretch. I've used my legs more than a lot of other people but they still take me where I need to go. I am truly thankful for that. I like to sit down on the floor and reach for my ankles. I do these stretches with my legs open and closed. I also lift my arms above my head and rotate my upper body. It feels nice to stretch in all sorts of directions.

CHAPTER 1:

From Age 100 to 101: 'Today's a good day.'

'If there's something you're worrying about, write it in your diary and your heart will feel refreshed.'

So says Granny Tetsuyo, who has written in her diary every night for the past three decades. Here is a glimpse of her everyday life.

GRANNY TETSUYO'S DIARY AT AGE 100
OCTOBER 2020: BE LIKE A HOE THAT NEVER RUSTS

October 1

Today I harvested some of the cosmos in the field. They're even taller than I am. I'm sure they gobbled up the fertiliser I'd sprinkled for my broad beans. I feel a bit mean saying this, but it's changed my opinion on cosmos! How cruel and greedy they can be despite their beautiful appearance.

The leafy vegetables have finally sprouted after I planted the seeds that Yori-chan [Yoriko Kaneku, sixty-seven, a local friend] gave me. Thank you. I'll make sure they grow up big and strong.

October 6

I made kashiwa mochi. I make them every May, but I was hospitalised for a month around this time due to the skin issues on my leg. Recently, I was looking at how big the leaves on the kashiwa oak tree in my front garden were. I kept telling Yori-chan about how wonderful they looked and she proposed the idea of making kashiwa mochi.

Kashiwa mochi is a simple Japanese treat with only three ingredients. First you get some anko [red bean paste], which you fold into some mochi [rice cake]. Then you wrap it in a washed kashiwa leaf before steaming it. We made some wonderful mochi that were neither too hard nor too soft. It was a joy to make them while chatting with Yori-chan.

OCTOBER 13

I asked my niece Nao-chan [Naoe Yokoyama, seventy-two, the third daughter of Yoshihide's older brother], who lives nearby, to come with me to take some money out at the Agricultural Cooperative for the first time. My heart was beating so fast and even now my hands are still shaking! It truly is convenient, but it does make me a little sad. Usually I talk to someone at the window to take money out and always walk out while saying many thank-yous and goodbyes. But at the Coop there was no one there. Your money comes out just like that and you leave without having said a

Happy on Her Own at 102

With her reliable niece Nao-chan, who helps her in her life alone.

word. What a cold experience! I love talking to people, so it was awfully lonely. When I talk to people, it turns into the energy that keeps me going.

OCTOBER 14

Nao-chan made me a lunch of chestnut and matsutake mushroom rice. The matsutake was cut into big pieces and placed right on top. It looked wonderful. I am truly lucky to have been made this feast. It is said that eating the first harvest will extend your life by seventy-five days. After this meal, my life was extended by seventy-five days … What to do?

OCTOBER 17

I hung up some persimmons to dry. The persimmon tree in the field always produces a large number of fruits, but I could only reach six of them. It's fewer than usual, but they'll be a great treat for New Year.

Happy on Her Own at 102

OCTOBER 19

When the weather's good, I pull up weeds in the field. I prepare the soil with my beloved three-prong hoe. I've been using it for almost half a century now, so the tips are a bit blunt and rounded but it's still going strong.

My hands are like my hoe. I've used them for so many years that their shape has changed. But ever since I was young I've always wanted to be like a hoe that never rusts. People get rusty if they're not doing something, don't they? If you continue to use your body, your head and your emotions, they'll never rust. This hoe is my life's treasure.

There are people who say that each day feels longer when you get older, but for me it's the opposite. I make my iriko sardine miso soup for breakfast, grapple with the weeds in the field, write my daily diary, if I've been given a present I write a thank-you letter, I wash my underwear and socks separately ... I remain grateful for each and every day and find joy in the small things. Days like these require a lot of the body and mind, so I sleep peacefully until morning.

October 21

Today is the anniversary of my husband's death. I suppose you could say that Yoshihide-san and I married out of love. He was a great teacher who worked earnestly and was respected by his students and their parents alike. I pay my respects at the Buddhist altar in my home every morning and evening. In the morning I simply put my hands together and pray, but at night I read out a sutra in a loud voice. I have a loud voice, so it's a waste if I don't use it.

Reading sutras is what my husband's family used to do before he passed away. He and my father-in-law would have a drink while my mother-in-law would recite the sutra in a loud voice. After she passed away, I took on that role. There are some days when I find it hard to gather the motivation, but I tell myself that my ancestors are waiting for it, so I make sure to do even a little bit each day.

NOVEMBER 2020: INSTEAD OF COMPLAINING, TRY AND STAY BUSY

November 1

Every day I go up and down the slope in front of my house. I use my hoe as a cane as I shuffle down the slope facing backwards. My shins aren't as tough as they once were, so if I went forwards, I'd probably come tumbling down. When my legs hurt, I focus on walking and count each step. I can make it down in around fifty steps. I think of this as a respectable form of exercise. This slope is like a barometer that measures how great I'm feeling. As long as I can walk down it, I'll be just fine. I enjoy my battle with that slope. And thanks to it, my heart and body stay strong. I face it with all my might.

When I'm coming down the slope, neighbours who pass by stop and watch over me to make sure I don't fall. How fortunate I am.

November 2

There was a cold rain today, so I stayed inside all day. My mood always drops on rainy days. It looks like I'm always singing life's praises, but I actually have my own share of worries. I share these worries with my diary and doing so makes my heart feel refreshed. I find myself making peace with them.

I thought I'd already put my troubles behind me, but maybe because I don't have any children, with each passing year I feel a little bit more lonely. When I'm alone in this house when the rain is falling, I can't help but think: *when my time comes, I hope I don't cause any hassle to anyone else.*

That's why I comfort myself by staying busy. I simply trick myself.

November 3

Today I headed out on Vroom [Granny Tetsuyo's mobility scooter that she bought when she was eighty-nine] to the gravesite. Our gravesite is located on the foothills of the mountain, so I putter along the ridges between the fields to get there.

Tetsuyo Ishii

I call it 'Vroom' because it gets me to where I need to get to in a flash. I often use it to get to the temple about 2km from home. My legs aren't as good as they used to be so they don't take me as far. Vroom is my partner.

November 5

I went to the hair salon today to get a perm. Someone I hardly ever see was there, so we got chatting and ended up losing track of the time. And then, oh dear, I forgot about my plans to go and see the autumn leaves with Nao-chan! She laughed it off and said it happens a lot, but I still feel very bad. My head felt nice and refreshed after my perm, but it seems like my brain was so relaxed that it got me into trouble. But if you waste energy complaining, you'll only weaken your heart and body. When I feel myself getting upset, I find a chore that needs doing and get my body moving.

November 6

I had my first ever flu jab. I don't think I'll get the flu, but from this year I'm going to a daycare centre once a week, so I need to get vaccinated. I'm not a big fan of injections.

November 8

I went with Nao-chan and some neighbours to Mitsuki Hachimangu Shrine in Mihara today. It was peaceful and the turning leaves were beautiful. It was a wonderful day. I first showed my appreciation for the happiness I had and prayed for it to continue. I also prayed for my family to remain healthy and to continue to live happy lives. A greedy request, I know.

November 12

Next Sunday an old colleague of my husband's is coming to visit, so I headed into Onomichi to buy some manju [a cake-like bun filled with a sweet filling] for him. It was a little bit pricey, but I found one I like.

Sometimes I buy myself a little treat when I make it into town.

I love manju, but I like all kinds of baked goods. My favourite is probably the anpan [a soft bun filled with red bean paste] you can get from Ogiropan in Mihara. They had a store right outside of the normal school I used to study at. When I lived in the dormitory, I usually had the spread of miso soup and mugi-gohan [barley rice], but on Sundays I would buy two anpan and some milk from Ogiropan in the morning. It was such a delight each week. Just thinking about it is making me want to go and get some.

NOVEMBER 16

Every month on the sixteenth there is a Buddhist wives meet-up at Daitsuji Temple [a Jodo Shinshu Hongwanji-ha temple that Granny Tetsuyo goes to]. When I arrive, I always go to the statue of Shinran and greet him by saying: 'Hello. Thank you for allowing me to visit today.' At home I recite sutras alone in front of the Buddhist altar, but at the temple today we all recited Shinran's *Shoshinge* together. My heart feels at peace when I sit in front of the Buddha. I also get to see everyone's faces. I always, always look forward to this day.

In the evening, I dug up my yams. My neighbours have all harvested theirs, but I was hoping that mine would get even bigger. I didn't water them enough, you see. I can't let myself get too lazy! Luckily, I got some wonderful yams. It felt like the earth was telling me, 'Tetsuyo, you're getting older but you're still working in the fields, so I'll help you out a bit.'

November 24

I'm drying some black soybeans. I'll be able to make osechi [a traditional meal eaten at New Year] with these. An indispensable tool in cooking these beans is rusted nails. First you make sure the nails are nice and clean and then wrap them up in some cotton, tied tight with some string. After you've soaked your beans for a night, you put them into a pot along with water, sugar, soy sauce, salt, some baking soda and the nails. You put a lid on and cook this all on a low heat for, let's see, around six hours. Long enough that you've forgotten about them and they'll be nice and soft.

Black soybeans are a favourite of mine. I handed out a bunch to my neighbours and this is all I have left, but it's more than enough. I look forward to eating them.

DECEMBER 2020: A LIFE WITHOUT HARD WORK IS A BORING LIFE

December 7

For the first time in a while, I saw the kids on their way back from school. They had got so big in no time at all and are already in secondary school. Come spring, one of them will be going to nursing school and the other to dental hygiene school. A lot of the children move out of town after secondary school. How encouraging they are. It's a wonderful thing.

When they were in primary school, I would stand at the bottom of the slope in front of my house and see them off. They all shook my hand before heading off. I'd grip their hands as tight as I could! I wanted to let them know that I hoped they'd be happy and do their best at school.

As they got older, they gripped my hand back more and more firmly. That made me really happy to see.

Sometimes when I oversleep and am not standing in the street, they'll ring the doorbell, worried about me. I rush outside and they'll say, 'Thank goodness!'. It makes me wonder if I'm watching over them or if they're watching over me.

There are fewer children now and I'll be seeing these kids off for the last time this coming March. That makes me feel a little lonely.

December 8

I wrote in my diary tonight too. I've been using this big three-year diary. I reflect on the people I met and what I did in the fields as I write in it after dinner. I'm reaching the end of my current diary at the end of this year, so I've prepared a new one. By the time I finish that one, I'll be 103, I suppose. I wonder what will happen? Well, I don't want to waste paper, so I need to live until then!

December 9

Today I thought of the past. When I was twenty, I started work as a teacher at a primary and secondary school. That was 1940, the same year that the Pacific War began. I was awfully busy back then, but I can vividly remember those early days.

Tetsuyo Ishii

During lunchtimes, I would bring a bench out onto a sunny corner of the school and sit the children down. One by one, I would clip their nails, fix up their hair, and wipe their runny noses. It was my daily routine. Back then their parents were so busy figuring out how to get by that they didn't have the wherewithal to take care of their children's appearances.

A lot of them had many siblings, and parents who were always busy with work, so they couldn't receive as much attention from their parents as they should. That's why I made sure to give each and every one of those children as much love as I could. As I held their hands or stroked their heads, I felt them relax and lean close. They were such dears.

I retired at fifty-six, but today one of my former students visited with his wife. I say 'former student', he's in his eighties now but when he's here, he turns into that little boy again.

In home economics, the children sewed trousers, but he couldn't do his very well. All the same, he stuck at it and finished it. Hard work becomes a driving force for children. When he was finished, I celebrated with him and praised him so much for his hard work. I have a lot of memories with him and we had fun chatting about them.

December 13

I had so many daikon radishes in my field. I don't pickle them like I used to and only harvest what I'll eat. Up you come! And what a huge radish this is. I can't pull it out all on my own. I told a visitor they could take it home, but I struggled pulling it out and the end snapped off! The other end is still in the ground, but I'll have that for myself.

December 16

A reporter from Hongwanji Temple in Kyoto [for the *Hongwanji Shinpo*, the bulletin for Jodo Shinshu Hongwanji-ha] came to do an interview. I suppose it's because I'm a one-hundred-year-old lady who loudly chants her sutras every night. They took a lot of photos. It'll only make the paper look shabby! I simply showed them my life as it is.

Tetsuyo Ishii

December 18

It's not yet the New Year, but I cooked up the black soybeans I had dried. They're known as 'hard work beans'. I eat them and pray for labours to come my way. There are some things you can only see or feel through hard work. You have to think about how to overcome the obstacle in your way.

A life without hard work is a boring one. Excuse my proselytising! It seems that no matter how old I get, I'm still a pro at nattering nonsense.

December 21

The paper today had a long feature about Sera High School's long-distance relay race, so I read it from top to bottom. I cheered them while watching the TV yesterday.

Nao-chan often drives me to Sera. I've seen them hard at work running. It brings a smile to my face to watch.

DECEMBER 22

I bought thirty New Year cards. More and more cards come in where the message says, 'I'm getting too old to write, so I won't be able to send a card from next year'. When I read them, I think, *But you can write!* and I feel a pang of sadness.

I've been writing, 'Let's try and keep our spirits lifted!'

FEBRUARY 2021: WORKING FOR THE JOYS TO COME

February 1

I'm so busy moving about every day that I write my plans on the calendar in the kitchen. When I look at the calendar, I can see the faces of the people I'm going to meet. I prepare my excitement for what's to come and face the day with energy.

Every Monday we have a Friendship Club meeting. We practise the taisho-goto [a Japanese lap harp-style instrument with keys that are like those found on a typewriter] with the local old ladies. Our repertoire is probably about forty pieces or thereabouts. Maybe we'll play *Kojo no Tsuki* [*The Moon over the Ruined Castle*] next time. It has a lovely timbre.

There are many days where we forgo practice. We gather around the heater to chat and laugh. It's so fun. After we chitchat, everyone goes home in high spirits.

The Friendship Club began in 1973. It's a very precious group that has been going for almost fifty years now.

The reason I began the Friendship Club was

because I saw all of the married women in farming families spending their days sat on the ridges between the rice paddies just staring into space. Around this time, farming tools were becoming more and more commonplace, and these women's grandchildren were now being taken care of by kindergartens, so they didn't know what to do with all the time they had.

That was when I decided that we should all get together. I was still a teacher then, so I got my baton and waved it as we all sang *Hato* [*Pigeon*, a Japanese children's song], with the women taking their frying pans, boxes, sticks, or what have you to beat the rhythm. Sometimes we had men come along and we did folk dances too. Some of the women took it as a chance to show off a bit and everyone smiled and laughed. It was like the springtime of our lives had come very, very late.

The first members of the club were older than me, born in the Meiji Period. They had worked so hard from a young age, singing lullabies or pulling up weeds, so never had any time for themselves. The Friendship Club was, in my eyes, something of a little revolution.

At the time I was busy too. I'd rush home from

school and work in the fields until sundown. I was trying so hard to be the model wife of a farming family, but now I'm living my life as freely as I choose without worrying about stepping on anyone's toes.

At lunchtime, my niece Nao-chan and I went to have some ramen at a local restaurant. I love the ramen in Onomichi. A few years ago I got chatting with the person on my table and we had a great time. I found out that their mother was also from Jogecho, like me. Each December, they send over some mochi. I'm a real chatterer but that lets me become friends with people quickly.

February 2

Today is Setsubun. In this festival, you throw as many beans as years you've lived, but look how many I've got! Both my hands are full. It reminds me that I've hit the milestone of one hundred.

When I think of each year of my life as a little bean, those years seem so loveable.

February 9

My kitchen has a sunken floor, so anyone can come in with their shoes still on. I put out some chairs and chat with my neighbours when they come by. I still have a chair that my father made eighty years ago for sewing machine work.

When I got married, I brought this precious chair with me from home. The sewing machine broke a long time ago, but the chair, which I use as a stool or to put my tea on, is still going strong.

It's a reminder of my father, so I can't ever part with it.

February 10

Wednesday is the day I visit the daycare centre. I've been going there for eight or so months now. Everyone else there is much younger than me, but I'm one of the newest recruits. In the morning, I say good morning to everyone and when it's time to sing, I sing louder than anyone. I also do the exercises with everything I have. It makes me happy to see everyone smile.

I also enjoy my baths there. Until last year, I used

Tetsuyo Ishii

my bathtub which is heated by firewood underneath, but now I take my baths at the centre. The bubbles feel great.

FEBRUARY 15

I do the laundry every other day. In the summer, I bought a completely automatic washing machine. I can't really work it out, which is a bit disheartening. Nao-chan said, 'All you need to do is press two buttons,' but sometimes it doesn't do anything after I press the button so I find myself growing impatient and pressing the other buttons. I end up telephoning

Nao-chan, telling her I couldn't get it to work, and she comes to help. This has been going on for about two months now.

FEBRUARY 16

I went to the morning and afternoon gatherings at Daitsuji. When I go to the temple, I always see people I recognise. I feel my spirit get stronger when I chant the *Shoshinge* [a Buddhist hymn] with everyone.

MARCH 2021: HOW I REACHED ONE HUNDRED YEARS OLD

Wow! A truly unexpected thing happened. On March 15, I was invited to speak at an event called 'Wisdom From Living One Hundred Years' held by the board of education in Onomichi.

I was a bit nervous in the waiting room, but as soon as it began my worries blew away.

The event began with everyone singing *Seto no Hanayome* [*The Bride from Seto*]. I said, 'Can everyone sing loudly for me?', before displaying a big piece of paper with the lyrics on them. I played the taisho-goto as accompaniment.

But saying I did a speech as a guest speaker makes me sound quite arrogant, doesn't it? I simply spoke of my life as an old woman who's been around the block a few times. The answer to the question posed by the talk is simple: how can I bring joy into my everyday life? That's all there is to it. The following are the five guidelines I gave during my short talk.

Happy on Her Own at 102

Five Guidelines to Living Well

1. Everything in life is merely two sides of the same coin. Focus on the positive side.

Everything in life has two sides to it. Look at this old woman's hands! You can see that the backs of my hands are covered in wrinkles, but turn them over and my palms are so smooth. You cannot understand things by merely looking from one angle. For example, even if you failed your college entrance exams and couldn't get into the university you wanted, you might encounter a friend for life at the one that you *do* go to. Flip failure on its head and see the good that has come from it. If you get caught up in failure, a sense of inferiority can take your life off course. It makes you into a small person. Failure is only a passing point; you can retry as many times as you like. There will come a day when you'll look back on it and view it as a success.

Tetsuyo Ishii

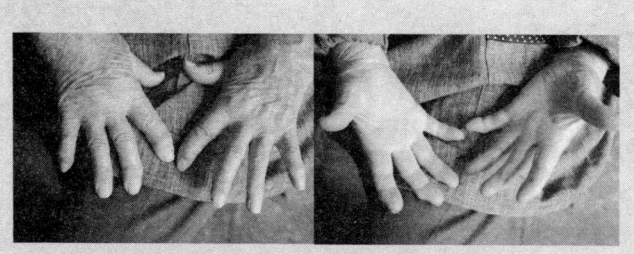

Everything in life is merely two sides of the same coin. Focus on the positive side.
The backs of my hands are covered in wrinkles, but turn them over and see how smooth my palms are.

2. Express your joy in abundance

If you always express your joy or your gratitude to someone, then it can easily seem like you're overacting. My niece Nao-chan often brings me food and my neighbours often help with cleaning – I suppose it's because they know how lonely it can be being alone, but I truly am grateful. I always openly express my joy whenever someone lends a hand.

I don't think it's good for us elderly folk to get short-tempered and quick to anger. The older generation needs to set an example for the young. We should be full of smiles so that they think, *Getting old seems kind of fun actually.* We need to be the ones who bring joy to, and cheer up, society. You only have one life, so I want to refrain from being a shrunken, gloomy person and live joyfully.

> **Express your joy in abundance.**
> Don't hold back when you say thank you.

3. Try to understand people

Back when I was the teacher of a Year 6 primary school class, there was this one boy who got awfully anxious when it came to maths class. I watched him and noticed that he was having trouble with his times tables. I took him to one side and said, 'You don't know your multiplication tables, do you?' and he burst into tears! His tearful face told me that he was embarrassed but relieved that I'd noticed. I took some time out to help him learn them. It was a really fulfilling experience for me.

I think my desire to learn about people, or maybe my tendency to observe them, is a hangover from my teaching days. Being an adult who is able to notice small changes in those around you – such as whether they seem to be low in energy, or don't seem to be eating well – is important. What you say is important too and can affect how they might react. If someone realises that you're looking over them, then they might feel relaxed and open up to you more readily.

Try to understand people.
Children have taught me a lot.

4. Turn negative emotions into smiles
It's easy to speak negatively. I've got nothing to eat. I've got nothing in my wallet. Why not swap out 'nothing' for 'nightingale'? I've got nightingale to eat!

Happy on Her Own at 102

I've got nightingale in my wallet! How silly it sounds and how easily you can transform 'nothing' into a smile. If you simply focus on the negatives, then you'll find your mood dropping with it. It's a quick route to feeling down. When you feel your heart starting to weigh down with negative emotion, you need to catch yourself and try and cheer yourself up.

> **Turn negative emotions into smiles.**
> Constantly focusing on what you don't have won't always help.

5. Learn from those who came before you

I found myself copying my mother-in-law without even noticing it. Just as she did, when I find myself with some free time, I weed the garden or field and make it nice and pretty. Even my nightly ritual of reading sutras in a big voice is a habit I learned from her.

I got married when I was twenty-six. At this time, my mother-in-law would carry a stack of firewood on her back and head into town to sell it. With the

Tetsuyo Ishii

money she earned, she would buy us sausages – a rarity at the time. She said they would be a grand side dish in mine and my husband's bento lunchboxes to eat at school. She always showed me how to approach work with a positive attitude, how to show you care for someone through little things. I think that everyone should find someone they look up to and learn from them. Copy them until it becomes a part of yourself. It will benefit you, I am sure.

Learn from those who came before you
Copying those you admire won't lead you astray.

APRIL 2021: FIND JOY IN REPETITION

April 1

A neighbour invited me to Miwacho in Miyoshi for some cherry blossom viewing. They were in full bloom and the riverbank was decorated by a whole line of them. Apparently the phenomenon of so many cherry trees in bloom is called 'senbonzakura' – one thousand cherry trees. This is the first time in my hundred years of life that I've seen such wonderful cherry blossoms. I couldn't help but say, 'Wow, wow!'.

I often go with this neighbour on drives with Nao-chan at the wheel. We stopped off at the Roadside Station Sera for some shopping. It was a lovely day.

April 2

I began the day with some weeding. I'm thinking of planting sweet potatoes in the plot where all the tall cosmos are. As I thought about it, I found the task became easier. I'll make sure to roast the potatoes, come autumn.

April 5

Hospitalisation

My foot suddenly started hurting so I asked Nao-chan to take me to the hospital [Mitsugi General Hospital in Onomichi]. Apparently I had a skin condition on my lower legs called 'cellulitis'. It has made my lower legs swollen and red. It itches and is too painful to walk. I need to let the doctors take care of me and help me get better.

April 16

It doesn't hurt much if at all anymore. With the pain gone, I can't help but worry about the weeds in my field. I want to go home as soon as I can. How quickly my mood changes. Staying in bed all day rusts my body and makes me feel down. I tell myself that I'll need to make sure I make the right preparations before I'm able to head out into the field again. I want to leave hospital and return to my daily life as soon as I can, so I need to be conscientious and do my rehab properly. Walking and exercising my mind does wonders in making me feel better.

Earlier, I played the piano in the rehab room. I played some songs I learned when I was teaching: *Medaka no Gakko* [*School of Medaka*] and *Tulips*. They're very easy pieces, but people always put in the effort to sing when there's a piano accompaniment. I was really happy when some of the other patients there sang along.

April 17

Due to Covid-19, the hospital doesn't allow visitors. My mobile phone is my sole lifeline for contacting anyone outside. I usually forget about it and it ends up running out of battery, but while I'm in hospital I often receive calls from Nao-chan and so I've been using it a lot. I'm in bed most of the time but my appetite is as strong as ever. I eat every last bite. Eating, sleeping and chatting are my special skills.

April 20

Discharge from hospital

My niece Yayoi-san [Yayoi Sakanaga, sixty-eight, lives in Jogecho, the daughter of Tetsuyo's younger brother] came to pick me up and I was able to leave the hospital.

The scenery was different to how it was before I was hospitalised. The green of the mountains is darker than before and people are transferring the rice seedlings into the paddies. As soon as I got home, I swept the fallen leaves from the garden, headed inside to the Buddhist altar and told Yoshihide-san, 'I'm home.' Yes, this is the place I need to return to.

I do the same thing most days, but I realise now just what a blessing that repetition is. A little lesson for me before I turn 101.

April 23

Hospitalised again
My legs felt funny again. Maybe I'm just being a little wimpy. I need to take care of myself.

WORDS FROM THE NEWSPAPER (PART 1)

It was four days after the cherry blossom viewing party that I received a message from Nao-chan, telling me that Granny Tetsuyo had been hospitalised. I was worried, but she told me, 'If all goes well, she should be discharged in two weeks or so.'

To prevent the spread of Covid-19, the hospital are not permitting visits. All the same, I wanted to know if Granny Tetsuyo was okay. Is she happy? Is she eating well? On the 9th, people at the hospital organised it so that she could peep her head out of the window up on the first floor. 'Tetsuyo-saaan!' I shouted and she leaned out with a big smile on her face. She lifted her hands over her head to form a circle to let us know that she was okay. We were relieved.

We considered putting her feature on pause for this month, but I wanted to tell our readers just how Granny Tetsuyo was taking this unexpected occurrence and how she was tackling it. I asked the hospital if they could take some photos of her during her stay and they gladly agreed. We featured some photos taken by the physiotherapist during her rehab and some before her dinner.

To no one's surprise, Granny Tetsuyo was optimistic about it. Over the phone, she kept saying, 'I want to return home as soon as I can.' It was clear that the hospital staff were taking care of her and she was doing her best to get better.

All the same, during the latter half of her stay, Granny Tetsuyo's tone when she spoke got a bit darker. She told us that sometimes she would wake up, unsure whether it was morning or evening. 'I need to be more realistic about all this,' she said, as if berating herself.

On the 20th, after around two weeks in the hospital, Granny Tetsuyo was discharged. We went to see her after this and recorded her condition on film. However, on the night of the 23rd, she wouldn't answer her home phone. We rang her mobile and finally got through. She picked up and said in this quiet, guilty voice, 'I'm in the hospital right now.' She told us that her legs had felt a bit painful and so decided it would be best to err on the side of caution and go back in.

She probably feels rather disheartened. This isn't the everyday life she grew so accustomed to through a century of life. Every day she would fold up her bedding and confirm that today too she was doing okay in mind and body. Her life alone is precious to her; something that she worked hard to maintain.

Tetsuyo Ishii

'I'm sorry for worrying you,' she murmured to me. I found myself apologising. Maybe our desire to see her better had caused her to rush her stay in the hospital. I told her that this time she should take as much time as she needed and to get better slowly and steadily. April 29th was Granny Tetsuyo's birthday – she turned 101.

MAY 2021: YOUR MOOD DEPENDS ON YOURSELF

May 24

I'm sorry for worrying you all. I have been discharged from the hospital now. I'm currently staying in my niece Yayoi-san's house near my family home in Jogecho. While here I have been helping weed their field, playing with Ko-chan [Yayoi's grandson, Konosuke, eight years old], and doing rehab with an intent to return to my home before long.

To tell the truth, this past month did quite a number on my heart. I got awfully wimpy. I was hospitalised twice and caused so much hassle for those around me. I know that dwelling on negative emotions is bad for you, but I was so crestfallen. I couldn't help but think of the possibility that this time would be the time that I would end up in a home.

If I'm being honest, I want to return home as quickly as I can. I know that I'll be okay living alone once more. But I also know that if I'm too greedy about having things my way, it will inevitably cause problems for my family and friends. I told them that

Happy on Her Own at 102

I was ready to give up on living alone and go into a nursing home. But Yayoi-san told me, 'It's okay. We'll support you.' I was so happy to hear those words. I thanked her.

I felt the clouds lift from my heart. I was filled with a desire to head home when I could and get into the field. It's strange. I suppose it's my body's way of telling me that I can keep on going.

My everyday life has been quiet and peaceful and my experience in hospital taught me how precious that is. Life doesn't always go how you expect and your body responds to that and changes. You need to respond to that and change your living circumstances in kind. I can get downhearted quite easily, but I have decided to accept the changes that will come. I want to remain flexible in responding to this. I need to train myself up still, it seems.

Before I knew it, I turned a hundred. Wait a second, I'm 101 now. Wow – how incredible indeed! The year I turned one hundred, I had a heavy weight in my heart all throughout the New Year period. I was about to hit the triple digits. Thinking that the year would bring me to one hundred put quite the strain on me.

Granny Tetsuyo with her beloved hoe.

Harvesting cosmos in her garden.

Viewing Sakura in the Spring.

With her niece, Yayoi-san.

At friendship club, which has been running for over 25 years.

I received so many letters from the readers of the newspaper. How fortunate I am to have met so many people this year.

Granny Tetsuyo aged nine, and on her 101st birthday.

Playing piano is one of Granny Tetsuyo's greatest joys.

Granny Tetsuyo's scooter, Vroom, is her favourite way to get around.

Tetsuyo Ishii

It felt like a real, irrefutable sign that I had gotten old. I didn't think that one night, going from December 31 to January 1, could bring with it such unease in me. I wonder if everyone else feels the same way?

I often tell myself that it's a waste not to live with joy in this life. You can brush off an unpleasant mood by simply changing how you approach it. In particular, in the past decade, I have made sure to listen to people in a calmer way. I can't wait until I can head back home and chat with them there once more. A lot of people have been ringing up Nao-chan, asking if I'm okay, so I'm grateful to be heading back.

Feeling pathetic, feeling down, that's still part of you. It's up to you whether you drag these emotions along behind you, or if you cut them off. You are the only one who can take care of your heart. I want to remain ever diligent no matter how old I get.

My 101st birthday makes me feel like I'm having my first birthday again. It's a second starting point for life. I feel I can keep on going. I shouldn't ever limit myself. I'll approach everything I do with everything I have. Next month, if I'm safely back home, then I need to start planting the sweet potato seeds.

Happy on Her Own at 102

Whenever she heads out, Tetsuyo always walks on the spot to warm up.

Tetsuyo Ishii

Words from Yayoi-san

I've watched my aunt from her side and have always respected how she lives her life. When I showed up to a Friendship Club (which my aunt created) meeting in the past, I noticed there was a piece of paper up on the wall of their meeting place. On it were the names of all the Club members' close friends and family who had passed away. I asked them about it and they told me that once a year they recite sutras for them and then reflect on their memories of their loved ones. This moment told me how much my aunt loves the people of our community.

Neighbours and former students are always visiting my aunt. I think a home where friends can easily come in and say hello is a wonderful thing. It's a truly blessed thing to live somewhere surrounded by neighbours who value one another. I want to respect my aunt's wishes and help her live her life how she has until now. I have experience with caring for my parents-in-law and I know that she has the energy to keep on living at home. Don't worry, it would be a waste for her to go to a nursing home already.

I want her to be the one to tell me when she can't

manage by herself anymore and if she wants to go into the care of a home.

WORDS FROM NAO-CHAN

Aunt Tetsuyo is a good listener. No matter how old she gets, she remains so curious and will listen to whatever you have to say. Before she was hospitalised, I showed her a great purple emperor caterpillar in the back garden and she asked me so many questions about it. She can make a conversation with anyone fun.

Of course, my aunt has her own worries. Because she never had her own children she has instilled in herself the firm desire to take care of herself by herself for as long as she can. I think in that respect she has a different attitude and resolve to getting older. She always maintains a good attitude so that she can continue living as best she can. I want to learn from her. She's such a good example to follow.

GRANNY TETSUYO'S DIARY AT AGE 101
JUNE 2021: CHERISHING DAYS SPENT ALONE

June 1

I had stayed at Yayoi-san's house to recuperate, but I was finally able to come back home and start my life alone again.

Today I used my bamboo broom and swept the garden. I really had been gone for a long time. The garden was covered in weeds and fallen leaves.

I hadn't been home long at all, but I planted some sweet potato sprouts in the garden. I made my morning miso soup and headed out on Vroom to my field. I've been doing this and that to keep myself busy. Or rather, I want to do the same things, or at least close to, as I did when I was well and healthy.

When I move my body, I work up an appetite. I sleep well. Very good – I need to keep at this pace. As I check how my body and energy levels feel, I cherish these days on my own. When I keel over one day, then that will be that. All I can do is live as well as I can until then.

WORDS FROM THE NEWSPAPER
(PART 2)

I heard that Granny Tetsuyo had been discharged from the hospital, so I went to visit her. I was looking at her bookshelf and picked up a Buddhist book without much thought when what I saw made the breath stop in my throat. On the reverse side of the cover, Granny Tetsuyo had written something: 'To my ancestors, I'm sorry. To Yoshihide-san, I'm sorry.' She had written this two years ago when she was ninety-nine.

Granny Tetsuyo married the late Yoshihide-san in 1946 but never had any children. This was an age when it was expected to have children. How heavy it must have weighed upon her to not be able to have any. Granny Tetsuyo faced this pain once again at ninety-nine and the questions that it implied. What should she do with the house? How should she meet the end of her life? With no children to rely upon, she wrote her internal struggles upon this page. It was plain to see that she wished to escape from this pain by apologising to her ancestors and her husband.

I'm certain that Granny Tetsuyo isn't the sort of person to turn away from these questions, from this 'homework' of life. I'm sure through writing out these thoughts, she will work through and manage it. It almost feels like I've been given my own 'homework' to reflect upon.

I asked Granny Tetsuyo if it was okay to talk about these thoughts of hers in the paper and she said yes. 'My heart's like the moon. Sometimes it's bright like the full moon. Sometimes it's like the crescent moon with a small part missing. I'd like to be like the moon and show my weaker side too to help anyone who may read all this.' Yet again, she responded to us with another nugget of wisdom.

OCTOBER 2021: LEARNING TO LET GO

October 6

It has been a long time since we last spoke. Since then, I have begun some medication. Look at what I've stuck to my fridge. It's a calendar into which I can put my medication. Great, isn't it? What a convenient thing this is. I've never had a single pill of medication in all 101 years of my life, so Yayoi-san prepared this for me so I wouldn't forget to take it.

October 7

My field is right in front of the bottom of the slope next to my house. Today I harvested my sweet potatoes. I cut them into thin slices and cooked them in my frying pan. They were so sweet and delicious. How wonderful! Oh, recently, something great happened. I now have a partner who helps me in the fields! He's a relative who lives nearby and was a teacher like me. I've known him as 'Kanamaru-sensei' [Junji Kanamaru, seventy-three, former headteacher at Mihara Middle School (affiliated with Hiroshima

Happy on Her Own at 102

University)], but he's an earnest sort who says that he knows nothing about farming so calls himself my apprentice. I'm really grateful for the help.

I've been thinking since I turned 101 that weeding and planting seeds and sprouts is tough on my own. But when I'm chatting with Kanamaru-sensei, it seems like nothing at all. How strange. I feel my spirits get lighter. From here on out, I'd like to start offloading those heavy weights I've been carrying all by myself up until now.

In the field with her partner, Kanamaru-sensei.

Tetsuyo Ishii

October 10

It's still hot. I stayed in the shade today as I went around the house pulling up weeds. After the day's work, I washed my feet in some hot water. In April, my feet swelled up and I had to go to hospital. Now, I need to keep them nice and clean so that nothing bad happens again. Until I was ninety-nine, I heated up the water with firewood for my baths and they were so lovely and warm. I'm heading to the daycare centre two times a week now and I can't wait for my bath there.

October 12

I often leave stacks of half-read books on my table. Sometimes I read them after dinner. Right now I'm reading the *Tannisho* [a 13th-century Buddhist text said to be written by Yuien, disciple of Shinran]. I'm reading through it as I look for parts that really resonate with me.

October 18

The 21st is the anniversary of Yoshihide-san's death. I got on Vroom and headed to the cemetery and did some cleaning. I can't stand up for long periods of time now, so I placed a sake bottle box in front of the grave for a chair. I got through the cleaning lickety-split. I'll leave the rest to my nieces. The grave is quite big, so I wonder if he's saying, 'Hurry up and join me!' I think it's probably more likely he's thinking, *Why are you so loud? Leave me in peace!*

October 19

I began a food delivery service in June and they brought me a ream of side dishes for dinner. Every day is such a feast I almost feel bad.

Until now I had prepared iriko sardines and stir-fried some leafy greens, occasionally using ingredients given to me by my neighbours. It makes dinner a lot easier to do.

NOVEMBER 2021: SPENDING THE END OF MY LIFE IN A CHEERFUL AND CHARMING WAY

November 1

Do you know who this is in this photograph? It's me at around age eighty. I remember I had my hair done up at the salon because I was reading the memorial address at a funeral at Daitsuji Temple. Someone snapped my photo. I'm wearing black and it's a nice photo so I thought it would be good for my own funeral, so I put it in this frame.

More and more people are preparing their funeral photograph before they pass on, but I think I was a bit of a trendsetter when I chose to do this. Although, I'm a bit too young in this photo. I didn't think I'd live for twenty more years. Sadly, I won't be able to use it anymore. If I did, the people who came to my funeral would say, 'Who's this then?'.

November 4

Yayoi-san visited me today. She always comes to check up on me and helps me with washing big things like my bed sheets or cleaning up. I did my laundry before Yayoi-san arrived – I need to do what I can do, after all.

In the afternoon, she took me out to the shops. I had a sudden craving for a hearty dish with some meat in it. Then I saw that some Kagoshima beef was half price. I can't get beef from my field, so I bought it. I bought some mezashi sardines too. In the past, I often ate ones that had gone brown, but the ones you see recently look rather delicious, don't they?

Tetsuyo Ishii

November 8

My neighbour Yori-chan [Yoriko Kaneku, sixty-seven, a friend] and Fumi-chan [Fumiko Teraya, eighty-three, another friend] came over and we made kashiwa mochi together. It's a real favourite of mine. There are some great leaves in the garden and whenever I see them, I feel like having some kashiwa mochi. In the past, I made kashiwa mochi on May 5 and arare [bite-sized rice crackers] on March 3. They were precious treats when I was a child. I'd put my freshly made arare into a paper bag straight from the pan and eat them little by little.

November 14

The potatoes that Kanamaru-sensei and I planted aren't getting very large. Kanamaru-sensei is terribly concerned, but a potato is still a potato even if small. It will be fine. I've been working the fields for years now and sometimes things don't go well. I'm self-taught, so I don't really know why that may be. Sometimes your potatoes want to grow large and sometimes they don't, I suppose.

November 17

I found a lot of my notebooks in the Buddhist altar and my drawers. Around the time I took that photo for my own funeral, I was losing a lot of my friends and former classmates. I went to a lot of funerals and so at the time, I wrote a lot about preparations for my own funeral service and how people should communicate with the temple. I natter and potter about cheerfully during the days, but at night I sometimes think about how I don't want to be a hassle for my nieces. I write my thoughts then in these notebooks.

I write scraps of thoughts in them, so I don't know how many books I've filled by now. Hmm, five, it seems. It feels like I'm just flinging my personal concerns at them, but I'd like to condense it down into one notebook and let them know.

November 22

I leave the rice fields to a neighbour, but we had our first harvest of the year. You can really taste the difference. I usually cook up four portions of rice at once and eat them in parts. I eat them in three or four goes, so I'm lucky that my appetite is still as healthy as ever. My weight? It hasn't changed from what it's always been, about 45 kilos.

WORDS FROM THE NEWSPAPER (PART 3)

Every time I meet with Granny Tetsuyo for an interview, I can always sense her love for a certain someone. After all, she always mentions his name at least once each time I visit her: Yoshihide-san, who passed away back in 2003. She looks up to the sky and thinks of him.

'I wonder if he'll praise me and tell me I gave this life my all.'

The absolute peace of mind that comes from the knowledge that the person she loved the most is watching over her helps sustain Granny Tetsuyo.

But I found out recently that's not all. Granny Tetsuyo had stood a picture of Yoshihide-san up on the drawers near her bed, but recently she's placed it next to her pillow.

Happy on Her Own at 102

I asked her, 'Did you put him nearer to you because you miss him?'

She replied, 'I'm doing this so that Yoshihide-san knows that *I'm* thinking about *him*.'

Yoshihide-san watches over her, but she also watches over him.

'Kue-issho' is a Buddhist teaching that says you will meet with someone again in the pure land. Granny Tetsuyo imagines her reunion with Yoshihide-san in the afterlife and tells us, 'I've got so many more wrinkles now. What will I do if he doesn't recognise me and walks right by?' Her shoulders slump down, but then she chuckles to herself and says, 'No, he'll probably recognise my big voice. Maybe I'll meet him singing.'

I can't help but laugh too. She talks about things after she's gone, but she's not gloomy in the slightest, rather full of life as she imagines what's to come. I sense a faint glow from her, the kind you get from someone who has lived a full life. I learn from her that death isn't scary but merely something that lies after life.

'Who knows, maybe he's found someone nice on

the other side,' Granny Tetsuyo says, occasionally showing an adorable jealous side. She tells us that although she's not written this in her After Death notebooks, she's told her nieces to put extra effort into her makeup for her funeral.

DECEMBER 2021: CHATTING ABOUT THE GOOD TIMES WITH FRIENDS

December 8

Today was a Friendship Club meeting with the ladies at the assembly hall. We started it back in 1973, so it really has been going on for a long time. Today was our annual Day of Consolation.

The reason we began the Day of Consolation was because of a sudden parting with one of our dear members. A member of the Friendship Club passed away in a sudden traffic accident in 1987. We didn't get to say goodbye or thank you. We all chatted about our shared memories and consoled one another. That was the start of the Day of Consolation.

When one of our friends passes away, we now add their name to a list that we write on the back of some wrapping paper. As you can see, there are many names of Friendship Club members and their family. Each year we write the names of those we lost in the past year and now the list is sixty-four names long. We pin up the paper and we all recite sutras with loud voices. After that, we gather around a wonderful spread of food and share our memories of the people on the list. We never run out of things to talk about.

Miyoko-san was really good at the taisho-goto [a Japanese stringed instrument]. She was like a pianist and always played with such emotion. I can see her now. We recreate those gestures of our dear friends and, like pulling precious memories from a treasure box, we share various episodes. Everyone says that it's like they're there with us. When the excitement calmed down and things got quiet, someone muttered that they wished they could hear her voice again.

When someone dies, that isn't the end. We remember them in our hearts. I want you to know that your friends who shared the same place and time as you will always remember you. Memories are proof that someone lived.

There is a limit to how much sadness one person can bear at a time. That's why we share that burden together and support that person's deep sadness. On the Day of Consolation, we come together to face sadness together and overcome it.

In the afternoon, someone from the Onomichi Town Hall came and took a video to be played at the coming-of-age ceremony this coming January. This was the second recording after they came last week and they asked me to give a message for all the kids who are coming of age. Twenty years old. What a wonderful age. It was a long time ago now, but I was twenty once too.

December 9

I harvested the potatoes with Kanamaru-sensei. He was worried that they wouldn't be too big, but those worries were cast aside. We dug up the potatoes and separated them into bags by size. I'll be eating the smaller ones first as they're more annoying to peel. If I don't do that, then there will only be little ones left that I won't end up eating! I don't want to waste food so it'll bother me if I don't eat them all. My mindset from growing up poor remains.

December 13

It's gotten awfully cold, so I brought out the space heater. I filled the tank up with kerosene. It was a

Happy on Her Own at 102

bit heavy, but I didn't mind as I thought of it as a little exercise.

DECEMBER 16

My niece Nao-chan brought over a little saucepan with some curry that she made. It was my first curry in a while. What a wonderful taste! I felt my body get warm and fuzzy.

DECEMBER 20

It's not New Year yet, but I made some karauma. It has been a staple of osechi [a traditional meal eaten at New Year] since I was a little girl. Oh, you've never heard of it? It's a sweet and spicy stir-fry of burdock root and iriko sardines. It's a variation on a kinpira gobo – a stir-fry generally made with carrots and burdock root. I add in some chillies for a spicy but sweet kick. As for the iriko sardines, I shred them with my hands and mix them in. They're full of nutrients and I really like it. We used to grow burdock root. Just like with the potatoes, the smaller crop always ended up getting left behind. But of course we couldn't throw it away, so we made heaps of karauma to use them up!

What's that, you think I'm a good cook? I don't really make anything fancy. Since I was young, I snipped out any recipes I liked in newspapers and magazines and stuck them into a notebook. I've got a bunch of recipes on making black soybeans alone.

Before lunch, Nao-chan came and brought a cake. She said her friend baked it and she did the cream and toppings. It's so wonderful that it seems like a waste to eat. I'm going to have it with everyone in the Friendship Club, but I'd like to taste the cream.

CHAPTER 2:

Tell Us More About Yourself, Granny Tetsuyo!

Granny Tetsuyo answers a number of questions sent in by the readers of the *Chugoku Shimbun* during the serialisation of her day-to-day life. In them she shares a number of memories about her childhood. These stories are like a path that allows us to follow the story of her life.

Could you summarise your aspirations for 2022 in one word?

Do I have to write it out with a calligraphy brush? Oh my, this is a little embarrassing! I suppose I'll choose the word 'laughter'. I spent a few weeks in hospital the year before last and last spring, so I'd like it to be a healthy year. I would like to laugh with my friends. That's all I wish for.

It's been a while since I wrote with a brush. I'll use this brush with its wonderful tip. I used to have this old, well-used brush that I brought to school, which was so rounded that I used to call it a club-brush. No one can improve their calligraphy with a brush like that. Or at least, that was the excuse I used to give. All the same, I love to write.

I sent out a lot of New Year cards this year. It's my yearly announcement to tell people that I'm still alive.

Tetsuyo Ishii

Filled with the wishes to laugh a lot with her family and friends this year.

Happy on Her Own at 102

Are there any books that have stayed with you?
There was this magazine called *Yonen Club* that was published by Kodansha. My father bought it for me every month when I was in primary school. My brushes and stationery cases were always old hand-me-downs, but books were the one thing he always bought for me. I think one volume was around forty-five sen. My pocket money was fifty sen, so I would get five sen for myself leftover. I stored them safely, folded in a newspaper.

I also looked forward to when my brother, nine years older than me, would come back from his lodgings and buy me a book as a present. I liked *Robinson Crusoe* in particular and read it so much I could recite it by heart. I would get so lost in reading that I'd abandon my household chores and my father would scold me. I still read in secret. I think when I was first given a book, I felt like I'd become an adult. I think that was the reason I became a book lover. I also read historical fiction like Eiji Yoshikawa's *Musashi*.

Tetsuyo Ishii

What do you think of when you hear the word 'love'?
First, my parents. Next, my husband. Our family was poor so I helped around the house from a young age, but I never thought of it as a burden. My father's name was Kongohei and my mother's name was Chika. I can still see them in my mind's eye.

I don't think either of them ever thought that their photograph would make it into a book!

They gave their everything to their work and raising me with love. The time spent living with parents who love you is irreplaceable.

What's the meaning behind your name?
My family name before marriage was Ogawa. You can write the kanji for it in six strokes: 小川. In the area where my family used to live, there was this superstition that if your given name had fewer strokes than your surname, you would live a better life. My father worried about this – after all, six is quite the small number. However, apparently ten strokes counted as zero, so he decided upon 'tetsu' (哲), which had ten strokes, and 'yo' (代), which had five.

I have three siblings. My older brother Taketo, my younger brother, Satoshi, and my younger sister, Momoyo. The first character of all of our names has ten strokes.

As for Tetsuyo, it gives off a tough, strong image, doesn't it? The 'tetsu' in my name means 'clear' or 'smart', but there is another 'tetsu' which means 'iron'. Sometimes I receive letters with this character instead! That makes me seem even tougher, doesn't it? But my father told me it was a good name, so I have no reason to doubt him. I've had it for 101 years, so I've grown very used to it.

Is there anyone you would like to meet right now?
I'd like to chat with Takushi Tanaka-san from the comedy unit, Ungirls. When I first became a primary school teacher, I was sent to work at Yoshino Ordinary Elementary and Junior High School in Jogecho [present day Fuchu-shi Jogecho]. Apparently, Tanaka-san's family are from the same catchment area, so I feel a sense of closeness to him. We're from the same place. I can't say I know many of his unit's jokes, though.

Tetsuyo Ishii

Tanaka-san's often on TV, going to this and that place. Was it *Motonari* (RCC Broadcasting) [a local variety TV show] that he stars in? Whenever I see him on TV, I feel like cheering him on.

What's your favourite colour?
It's purple. You might not believe it looking at me now, but I was quick on my feet and always first in the sprint at primary school. Back then, we'd have sports days where five or six of the local primary schools would compete against each other. The colour for my school, Jogecho Ordinary Elementary and Junior High, was purple. In the relay, we would have purple headbands. It was such an honour to run with one and I was so happy doing it.

I was always the first or final runner in the relay. I wasn't the best at studying, but I never lost when it came to running.

What's your daily pleasure?
Probably eating! During the cold season, like now, I like having warm soups. I had a mixed soup this morning with lots of daikon radish and three chunks of mochi. What's that, you think three is a lot? I can have six if I set my mind to it! Even past a hundred, I still get hungry. Mochi is one of my favourite foods, but I make sure I don't overindulge.

I have been using dentures since my sixties. Fortunately, I can still eat anything I like. I've never had any issues with them. The dentist really made me a good set; it fits perfectly to my mouth.

Granny Tetsuyo, I'm a secondary school girl and a big fan of yours! If you were seventeen again, what would you like to do?
This letter is from a seventeen-year-old? Wow, wow, how wonderful! Let me see, when I was seventeen, I was in my second year of normal school. I left my home in the countryside to live in the dorms and was surrounded by new people. I gave my all to achieve my goal of becoming a teacher. In particular, I did my

best to practise the organ. Until then, I had never been taught, I simply watched and copied.

Every week we would have a recital test where we had to perform in front of everyone else. The school had a few dozen organs, but there was a schedule so you couldn't practise unless it was your turn. I wanted to practise and get as good as I could, so I often went on the search for a free organ and did some extra practice. Back then, I could see myself improving the more work I put in. And each time I did, I felt myself getting more confident.

But if I could go back to seventeen again, I think I'd like to try the organ again with all I had. At the time it felt like a pain, but looking back on it, it was really fun.

Now, Yayoi-san has an electric piano at her house, so she lets me play. She has so much sheet music! Today maybe I'll play *Sen no Kaze ni Natte* [*I Am a Thousand Winds that Blow*; a Japanese translation of the poem *Do Not Stand at My Grave and Weep*, put to music by Masafumi Akikawa] and *Ue o Muite Aruko* [literally, 'I look up as I walk' and known in the West as *Sukiyaki*, a popular song by Kyu Sakamoto].

Do you have any favourite singers? What genres do you like?

I like Taro Shoji. I like *Akagi no Komoriuta* [*Akagi Lullaby*]. You haven't heard of it? He sings in this careful way, without rushing at all. I like songs that are sung seriously like that.

When we were young, everyone said that my younger brother had a great voice, so he often sung this song at concerts. Me? I didn't sing on the stage, but with the fields behind me. When I came back from school, I had my sister – seven years younger than me – on my back and I'd sing her a lullaby in a loud voice. I often sang songs we learnt in school when going to and from school.

Since I grew up, I've become a bit more reticent. I like any song. I've even penned some of my own songs – music and lyrics. I wrote a song about how wonderful Minogocho Nakano, where I live, is. It's called *The Nakano Song*. We sang it in the Friendship Club. Singing is wonderful. It makes your heart strong. All of those silly things you're worrying about go flying out the window.

Tetsuyo Ishii

What's your favourite season?
I like all the seasons in moderation. Whether it's hot or cold, every season has its own beauty. At the end of winter, sometimes it can start to get warm, but then suddenly it starts snowing. It's like the winter is saying it doesn't want to leave yet. How charming! When spring arrives after each cycle of the seasons, I wonder how many springs I'll see. I sounded a bit like a poet then, didn't I? How funny! How changeable the heart is. Even mine.

Is there anywhere you'd like to go?
Sometimes I find myself wanting to see the ginkgo tree in my alma mater. The school was called Jogecho Ordinary Elementary and Junior High, but now it's known as Jogekita Elementary School. I wonder how much older that tree is than me? It stands proudly near the school gates.

When I was in my fifth year and started running, I couldn't wait for practice after class. We'd gather under the ginkgo tree and do warmups. It wasn't just running practice, we'd listen to our teachers in the shade of the leaves. Whenever anything happened, people would come and gather at the ginkgo tree. It was a symbol of the school. When I look at that tree, I think of my childhood. I didn't have anything to worry about and every day was so fun. The town and the school have changed since then, but the tree has remained the same.

What does a normal day look like for you?
I wake up at around 6.30. The first thing I do is wash my face with some cold well water. Next, I give a prayer to the Buddha. I then cook up four portions of rice and prepare some miso soup. I cook rice once every two days. In other words, I eat two portions per day. It's gobbled up in no time.

At 7.30, I eat my breakfast. I usually watch the news on NHK or a serialised drama while eating. After that, I pop on my reading glasses and read the paper from cover to cover. I then wash up the dishes and do some other chores.

At around ten o'clock, I 'commute' to the field.

At noon, I have my lunch. I use up whatever I

Tetsuyo Ishii

have, whether that's tamagoyaki [a kind of omelette] and flavoured nori seaweed or kombu tsukudani [simmered seaweed].

In the afternoon, I have a little nap or reread the paper. After that, I head back to the field. It makes me happy because people who pass by often say hello. Usually we end up chatting and I get so lost in the conversation that the day has passed before I know it.

At 7 p.m., I have my dinner. Sometimes I have a bento from the food delivery or enjoy something brought by Nao-chan or a neighbour. I have baths twice a week at the daycare centre, so I wash my feet and legs. I then write in my diary, go to the Buddhist altar, then go to bed at 10. I sleep well. I don't wake up once until the morning.

Granny Tetsuyo, what's your secret to staying healthy?

If you don't use your brain, it will start to rust. Personally, I always have a dictionary close at hand. When I'm reading the paper or a book, if there's a word that I don't understand then I will always look it up. I just feel restless not knowing. I sometimes think that I probably study more now than I did when I was a teacher. I also asked my niece to buy me an arithmetic drill book so I make sure to keep my mind healthy by solving the exercises. I often get perfect scores.

But it's important to enjoy giving your brain a workout. One thing I've been particularly into recently is a game where you see just how many different kanji you can write for one homophone. For example, in Japanese we have the word 'kaki', but it can mean all sorts of different things depending on what kanji are used. So I'll write them down: persimmon, oyster, late summer, following text ... I like to challenge other people to see who can write the most. I get quite heated when it comes to a challenge, you know. I won't lose!

How do you deal with things that annoy you?
You shouldn't snap back while your feelings are still heated. You might feel better in the moment, but you'll regret it later. My mother used to say, 'Swallow the saliva in your mouth three times before talking.'

Tetsuyo Ishii

It's important to take a moment. If you do, then your emotions should calm down. Who knows, maybe you'll be able to get a cool head and think, *They're not a bad person, but now that they're this old, maybe this is something that won't change.*

What would you like your final meal to be?
What a difficult question! Hmm ... I'd be happy with anything, really. If I were to pick, then I'd say barazushi. I'm a big fan of vinegar. Maybe that's why my body's so flexible now? Anyway, it's a really colourful dish with its yellow egg and pink sakura denbu [dried cod flakes]. I get excited just looking at it. When I was younger, my mother used to make it for me when there was something to celebrate. When I have it now, I remember that bliss from my youth.

What do you write in your After Death notebooks?
I don't have children, so I've written various odd things in there since my eighties for the benefit of my nieces. When I think of something, I'll write it in a notebook

that's close to hand, so it's become a bit chaotic. I need to organise them at some point.

Anyway, I write anything, even minor things. Things like, I'd like for the funeral to be held at home, what presents should be given in return for funeral offerings, about what kimono I should be put in for the funeral. Oh, I've also been thinking of the chief mourner's speech. To relieve any effort or pain for whoever has to do it. By writing things like that, there will be nightingale to worry about. It takes a load off my own heart.

Tetsuyo Ishii

I don't hesitate in letting go of the things that I know I can no longer do. I cherish the things that I can still do, cheer myself on and turn those feelings into self-confidence that I can still do them.

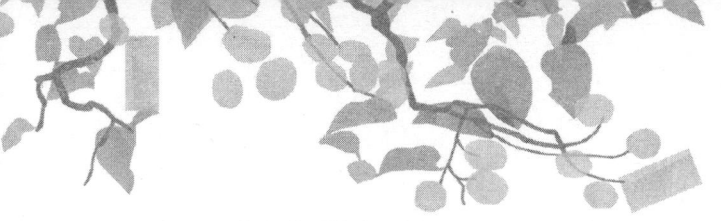

CHAPTER 3:

Grateful for Life at 102

At age 102, Granny Tetsuyo shares with us her secret to 'ageing well' and the five guiding principles for being true to herself.

CORRESPONDENCE FROM GRANNY TETSUYO

FEBRUARY 2022: HOSPITALISED DUE TO HER WEIGHT?

When everyone saw the picture of me from January, I received many worried messages that I'd put on weight or that my face was swollen. Do I really look so different? Well, the truth is, my legs have been feeling a little swollen recently.

I was seen during a regular checkup at hospital [Mitsugi General Hospital in Onomichi]. I was given some medication and told to see how things progressed at home. When I was walking up the slope to my house, I found it difficult to breathe. Apparently there was a strain on my heart. I didn't want to be going in and out of hospital, so I decided to be checked in.

Apparently it wasn't good for me to put on so much weight. I guess I had too many hearty meals over the New Year period.

After dinner, I found myself eating ohagi [a type of sweet rice ball] and then a choux bun. My appetite is as voracious as ever. But because it's been so cold,

Tetsuyo Ishii

I found myself slacking off from working in the fields or pulling up weeds. I put on 4kg in just one month!

I did my best and spent my stay in hospital without any snacks. My weight returned to its usual amount. Thank goodness I got better so quickly. I'll probably stay with Yayoi-san after I'm discharged and wait until spring comes around.

MARCH 2022: I'D LIKE TO KEEP ON LIVING HERE, DAY BY DAY

Unable to sit still

I spent the month after leaving hospital at Yayoi-san's house. She put me up in a wonderfully soft futon and made such delicious meals. Because I can't sit and do nothing, I sometimes help with the vacuuming, making dinner, or pulling up weeds on sunny days.

Oh, I've also been playing the electric piano for two hours every day. Do you know *Jupiter* [Ayaka Hirahara's debut song]? Yayoi-san had the sheet music, so I played it, and what a wonderful song it is. I practised a lot to play it perfectly. I had the thought that I'd like to play it for the people of Ukraine. I was in Jogecho during the Pacific War and witnessed the Fukuyama Air Raid. When footage from Ukraine plays on the TV, it's just so terrible I can't stand to watch. How shameful it is to wage war in this day and age.

Next month I turn 102. I imagine there aren't too many people who live alone at this age. It might appear like an adventure or some kind of challenge from the outside, but it's thanks to everyone who supports me that I can continue it without worrying. If I truly was on my own, then I'd probably be rather depressed. But my nieces are always there, watching over me. That relief becomes the energy that drives me forward.

Coming home

Eventually I was able to leave Yayoi-san's house and return home. My house and field were waiting for me. While I was away, Kanamaru-sensei was looking after them. It is really encouraging having his help. My house gets a lot of mice. Kanamaru-sensei put down some traps and said he caught two while I was away. He also told me that some monkeys were playing pranks in the field and pulled up most of my onions.

I can't remember when it was, but once I saw a monkey in front of the house. It had some soybeans under its arm and was just strolling by as if nothing was out of the ordinary. It hadn't noticed me, so was in no rush. As for me, I was so shocked and could only stand and watch!

I found some tree onions growing in my field.

A sign that spring is here. Maybe I'll take some and put them in my miso soup for lunch. I need to plant some potatoes with Kanamaru-sensei before March is over. I'll be very busy.

Out to the shops!

My fridge was empty, so I went to the local supermarket with Yayoi-san. I needed to get some tofu and abura-age [fried tofu] for my daily miso soup. While going down the aisles, I picked up some things that caught my eye. Today I bought some dried fish, amberjack sashimi, beef, sakura anpan [a soft bun filled with red bean paste and cherry blossoms], and some spring-like pink treats to offer to the Buddha. It's thanks to Yoshihide-san that I've managed to come home safely after almost two months away, including my hospitalisation. While Yoshihide-san, my nieces and my neighbours watch over me, I'd like to live in my way, day by day.

Tetsuyo Ishii

TV SHOOTING

Wow, wow! Apparently an old lady like me is going to be on the television, so someone from RCC Broadcasting [Kazuhiro Yamamoto, TV show producer, works on the TV show *Imanama!*] came over to do some shooting. He said I should act how I normally do, but I didn't know what to talk about. All the same, it's really lovely to meet these young people and talk about things. This is something I only got to do because I made it to 101! Everyone has taken such good care of me and what a good life it was.

Filmed for RCC's Imanama!

Happy on Her Own at 102

Oops! I can't say 'was', can I? What a good life it is. I'm still living it.

A RELIABLE CARE MANAGER

Yashiki-san, my care manager who always looks after me, came to visit. It seems that I'm the number-one person to be taken care of. She told me about various services they could provide so that I could continue living alone without worries. Apparently a new centre [a small nursing home with lots of facilities] will be opening nearby. They will send over some day carers from time to time and they say I can pop in and stay there if I like. I decided to go and see it with her. What a blessed age I live in!

Tetsuyo Ishii

APRIL 2022: THE SECRET TO AGEING WELL

I just turned 102.

This year, I enjoyed some cherry blossom viewing with my Friendship Club. I started the Friendship Club back when I was in my fifties. I don't feel like I've changed much from back then, but the fact is that on April 29, I had my 102nd birthday. I hope I can continue to do the things I like without troubling anyone.

The other night, as I was settling into bed, I fell asleep to the sudden thought of how grateful I am to be allowed to live this long. If someone told me I could become twenty again, I wouldn't want to. I know many people believe that there is value in youth, but I believe it's good to live well in relation to your own age.

I'm busy each day. I make sure I draw up a to-do list and work my way through it. By doing so, you can encourage yourself and take it as a barometer for your own health.

Recently, taking out and putting away my winter

Happy on Her Own at 102

bedding has become that daily barometer for me. I had thought, *As long as I can still do this, I'm fine*, but as I get older so too does my body. So instead of putting it away in the futon closet like I used to, I now simply just fold them up. It's a good and viable method! You should be aware of your limits. It isn't good to push yourself to do the impossible.

One thing that I do every day without fail is make miso soup. Today too I woke up and as I prepared it, I thought how good it was. Food you prepare yourself tastes wonderful because of that emotional depth. I don't hesitate to let go of the things that I know I can no longer do. I cherish the things that I can still do, cheer myself on and turn those feelings into self-confidence that I can still do them.

I think it was after I turned eighty that I started to let go of the things that were only taking up unnecessary space in my brain by me worrying about them. Yes, I started to give up a lot faster than I used to, but that's not a bad thing. If someone spoke badly of me, then I would simply feel a bit sorry for them. If someone only ever boasted and bragged, then I would simply let them be. I decided to put a lid on that ever-jealous part of my heart and instead put that energy into complimenting people. They are them and I am me. It is no surprise that there are differences. I decided that living a happy life would be satisfaction enough.

I don't overstrain, I don't embellish – I simply take things as they are. I don't make myself seem anything other than what I am. I would advise letting go of tiring things like jealousy or greed. In their place, enjoy fully what makes you happy or excited. All there is to that is to subtract the negative and add in the positive. After all, being happy and healthy starts with your heart. Your heart brings the rest of your body along with it. I think it's really important not to let your heart weigh heavy.

I also think that it's a waste not to enjoy the time while you're alive. I think there's a real joy in putting a voice to your emotions. Try saying it out loud: 'Ahh, I'm starving,' or 'Wow, that was a delicious meal!' If you're aware of each moment, then the day passes by just like that.

JUNE 2022: THE FIVE PRINCIPLES FOR BEING TRUE TO MYSELF

Recently, I feel like I've finally got a handle on how I can cheer myself up, but when I was younger I shouldered all of these worries and troubles. As a result I was often a bit spiky. Through various life experiences, coming to terms with their emotions, I think people smooth down the corners of their heart to become a lot more rounded. Of course I'm no exception. Here are some things that are important to me being true to myself.

The Granny Tetsuyo Way: Five Principles for Being True to Myself

1. Love myself completely
2. Protect my own tempo
3. Value time alone
4. Find satisfaction
5. Value even the smallest things.

Happy on Her Own at 102

Expressing joy at harvesting an extra-large potato.

People might think of me as quite free of worries because I'm always smiling, but in my youth I experienced many struggles. The first, after marrying Hideyoshi-san at twenty-six and joining the Ishii family, was the fact that I never had any children. My husband was quite the stoic warrior type and was village mayor back when this part of Onomichi was Minogo Village. I was the wife of a farming family

Tetsuyo Ishii

that went back generations and got married during an age when it was expected that you would have lots of children. I thought that if I couldn't have any children, then there wasn't any point in me being in the family at all.

I'm not sure if it's exactly correct to label it as mockery, but I just didn't want people saying things behind my back like, 'The Ishiis don't have any children, did you know?' I suppose I was viewing it as a personal failure. I channelled that energy into giving my all to my teaching work, cooking and the fields. I would leave school as fast as I could and head to the fields straight away. I was focused on making sure each day was so filled with work that I didn't have time to think about my worries.

But I think my teaching work did a lot in saving me. If I had been just a wife and nothing more, then I would have needed to be at home a lot. By being at school, I was able to have the joy of working with children and staying true to myself. I also got close with their parents. I think I was able to try my best at home because I had a place where I had a purpose.

It was true that Yoshihide-san was a hard worker

and many people looked up to him, but this popularity also meant that he would bring people over every night and drink a lot. The money I worked hard to earn would disappear, used to entertain others and provide their drinks. That was another reason I needed to work hard.

My work was important in giving me a sense of purpose. It helped protect my heart.

Looking back now, I was a little bit pitiful. When I retired to look after my parents-in-law, I felt a great weight falling from my shoulders. I realised then that I had been wearing this armour that didn't allow for any gaps.

I don't think that it was all for nothing. I am here now because I went through hardships and difficulties. I don't hate that former spiky version of myself. After all, that too was me. I want to accept and love myself completely.

Before Yoshihide-san passed away he told me: 'You don't need to worry yourself that we never had children.' I thought that it was a burden that I had been shouldering alone as the wife who married into the family, but he must have also taken on that burden with me. It was thanks to those words that I was able to refresh my mindset and heart. I think maybe it was because I had been so low that now that the weight is off my shoulders, I have so much joy in my life. You need to make sure you congratulate yourself for your achievements.

I can't move as quickly as I did when I was younger. Whether that's heading out to the field or preparing dinner, I need to make sure I take little breaks to kickstart the engine. After lunch yesterday I wanted to head to the field, but by the time I could get off my behind it was already getting dark! It wasn't as if I was doing anything while sitting on that chair in the kitchen. But I think that everyone has their own tempo. You need to act based on how you feel in each moment.

I love chatting with my neighbours and having fun with the Friendship Club, but this is an important time to spend by myself. I'll read a book or the paper, or, for most of the time, just sit with my thoughts. I suppose you could view it as recharging my battery so that I can restart my engine. This time is precious, it helps me continue to move at my own pace.

Happy on Her Own at 102

If you accept things as they are, your heart will feel lighter. There are many things I can't do now that I am 102, but I find joy in what I can still do. Even if the result isn't so beautiful, I think it's important to find satisfaction in accomplishing it.

Whenever I see the children coming home from school, I always make sure to say hello. I think about how they've spent the whole day studying there and they seem absolutely adorable to me. I often lose myself in these everyday scenes.

As the years go by, I start to wonder for how much longer I'll be alive. No one lives forever. Maybe that's why I want to be satisfied with this precious time as each year passes by.

CHAPTER 4:

Granny Tetsuyo's Tasty Recipes for a Long Life

We asked Granny Tetsuyo to tell us what she often cooks for herself. Each dish looks incredible and will be sure to help you live a long and healthy life. Try making some for yourself at home.

Kinpira with Iriko Sardines and Potatoes

Chop up the iriko sardines into easy-to-eat pieces and finely chop your potatoes and carrots. Heat up one tablespoon of sesame oil in a pot. Add a little salt and leave it for just a moment before stir-frying the iriko sardines and potatoes on a high–medium heat. When the potatoes start to go a bit see-through, add in the carrots. Once they're well fried, add some soy sauce. In my home, I always have a big pack of iriko sardines from Setouchi.

If you want another dish that uses iriko sardines, you can simmer them with some napa cabbage and add some soy sauce when soft. I recommend adding a splash of vinegar before eating. Iriko sardines and vinegar are both great for the body. This dish tastes similar to eight-treasure vegetables. I could eat it forever!

Tetsuyo Ishii

Bara-Zushi

Cook 600g of rice.

Finely chop lotus roots, carrots and shiitake mushrooms and add them to a pot. Add soy sauce, cooking sake and mirin and let everything simmer.

Add awase-su (a mixture of 80ml of vinegar, 2 tablespoons of sugar and 1 teaspoon of salt) to a pan and heat it up so that the sugar and salt dissolve. Add the rice and the other ingredients to the pan and stir.

Plate it up and top with kinshi tamago egg garnish (add a little sugar to give it a sweet edge), sakura denbu (dried cod flakes) and chopped shiso leaf.

You might find it a bit too vinegary, but I like rice that has been softened a little by the vinegar.

Boiled Flounder

Add equal amounts of cooking sake, soy sauce and mirin to a pan, one at a time. Add a little water then put in a cut of flounder. Turn up the heat to medium. Once it starts simmering, add some thickly shredded ginger.

In the past, a fishmonger from neighbouring Mihara used to visit so I often made fish dishes.

If you don't have flounder, this dish tastes great with dark-banded rockfish too.

Tetsuyo Ishii

Basic Miso Soup

Put a ladleful of water and six chopped iriko sardines into a pot and cook them on a medium heat. When it starts to boil, add some carrots and napa cabbage. Once the vegetables have softened, stir in the miso paste and allow it to melt. The iriko sardines don't only act as a stock, they are also tasty to eat. They're full of calcium. When the soup is ready, I like to top it with some finely chopped spring onion. You can make other variants with other vegetables. Sometimes I use the vegetables from my field.

I also like dropping an egg in and letting it get half-boiled.

Sukiyaki

Cut your beef into thin strips and stir-fry them on a medium heat with sesame oil. Add sugar, soy sauce, mirin and cooking sake to taste. Then, add in diagonally-cut slices of burdock root and bite-sized pieces of napa cabbage before simmering. I don't simmer the vegetables for too long as I like the napa cabbage still to have a crunch to it. Top with some finely chopped ginger for a refreshing taste. It makes me want seconds!

Tetsuyo Ishii

Cucumber Salad

Thinly slice your cucumber. Sprinkle it with salt and set aside for five minutes. When the salt has drawn out the moisture, massage the cucumber before giving it a big squeeze to get all the moisture out. All you need to do is mix it with some sugar and vinegar and it's ready. Put in slightly more sugar than you think you need. I love vinegar, so once I've eaten half of whatever else I'm eating – stir-fried veg or grilled fish – I add another dash of vinegar. The flavour changes as you leave it. Feel free to top with shiso or sesame seeds to your liking.

A Closing Message from the Paper

'We found our model example for those
living into their 100s.'
– *Yoko Kinomoto and Naomi Suzunaka,*
Chugoku Shimbunsha

This book is based on a portion of the serialisation in the *Chugoku Shimbun*, where we reported on Tetsuyo Ishii-san's everyday life. We captured the daily life of a hundred-year-old woman, picking up the words and phrases that she said. Both of us, two women aged around fifty, were in charge of the reportage. We visited Tetsuyo-san and got lost in our chats with her. Every time we visited, we found ourselves feeling so excited to share her wisdom with our readers. I think that it was the two of us who were the most encouraged by this whole experience.

Tetsuyo-san puts her absolute all into living. She puts her little body into action no matter what she does. She grits her teeth as she pulls out a daikon radish from the field. She plays the organ with a blissful expression. She leans forward when talking to catch every word. She pretends to wipe away the drool from her mouth to show her joy when a neighbour gives her a present of food.

She gave her all during our reporting too. For example, when we asked her to smile for the camera, she would always do something silly without us asking. When we told her we would be recording her voice for an interview, she would suddenly switch to a well-to-do tone. When we visit, she always keeps an eye on us and helps us out with all that she can do. It was clear to see just how much she values the people in front of her and we were moved every time.

As we entered our third year of reporting on Tetsuyo-san, we gradually understood the reasons

Tetsuyo Ishii

she gives her everything to whatever she does, even if she's not always aware of this herself. We found three important things to be learned from her.

The first is that your daily activities are a barometer of your physical and mental energies. This is something that Tetsuyo-san, who wants to live in her home for as many days as she can, believes in. When you reach one hundred, going into a nursing home is an option that you cannot ignore. All the same, she lights a fire under herself by announcing that she is the owner and master of her home. Without any children or grandchildren to inherit her home, she wants to live in her house for as long as possible and protect it with all the love that she has. This is her mission as the last one to take care of it.

'When I move my body, I work up an appetite. I sleep well. Very good – I need to keep at this pace.' Tetsuyo-san values her life alone while keeping track of how her body and mind are doing. She cannot let up, every moment is a serious battle: 'When I keel over one day, then that will be that. All I can do is live as well as I can until then.' She smiles while speaking so easily of her strong resolve.

Happy on Her Own at 102

The second is the fact that she wants to enjoy the joy of her independence: 'When you become old, it's easy to become a passive person. It becomes normal for people to give things to you or prepare things for you. It makes me want to ask them whose life they think they're living.' Comments like this show how strict she can be – to other elderly folk too.

Tetsuyo-san thinks of what she should do and what she should eat, then moves into action. If there is something she cannot do, it is then that she asks the help of someone who is capable. She doesn't hesitate to make use of the nursing service. For Tetsuyo-san, she quibbles less about 'independence' and more about 'self-control'. A common thing she says is, 'I'm alive too, so if I don't enjoy this life, then what a waste it would be.'

The third reason for giving her all to life is, we think, to encourage her own self. Normally, Tetsuyo-san is cheeky, cute and full of life, but sometimes she shows us another side to her: the loneliness of not having children, the loneliness of eating meals alone, the pain she feels on rainy days and a few tears start to flow. Tetsuyo-san often describes herself as 'wimpy' during these moments.

Tetsuyo Ishii

'When I sit down on my own without saying a thing, I find myself thinking about all sorts of negative things.' That is why she moves into action with all she has, both in her mind and in her body. She expresses abundant joy at small things and we are reminded that she's encouraging herself, so that her wimpy side doesn't rear its head.

In the first entry for our serialisation, we said, 'We found our model example for those living into their 100s.' Living long is a risk in our society today. We still feel a little timidity at the possibility of tripping over as we get older, but we now feel like we can enjoy our second start at life too. That's thanks to meeting Tetsuyo-san.

We head down the road in front of Tetsuyo-san's house after a day of interviewing. She continues to wave as we go. As we pass by her house again in the car, we see that she's still waving. 'Take care on your way home!' she yells. We feel a rush of relief at her loud voice and tears threaten to come to our eyes with our desire that she remains healthy for a long time to come. We shout back, not willing to lose to her.

'We'll be back soon, Tetsuyo-san!'

Aspirations for 2023

It's 2023. This spring I will turn 103. I'm doing just great this year too, thank you.

What's that? You want to know how I will spend this year? I don't intend to aim too high. I want a year with no issues. I want to find happiness in the ordinary, peaceful everyday.

When I think about the time I have left, each and every moment seems so precious. That's why I want to put that little bit extra into my life on my own. At the end of it all, I want to think, 'Ahh, I lived. That was a good life.'

I hope all of you continue to live without any issue

too. I pray for a peaceful world without war. I pray for all the children in the world to be able to live peacefully. These are the wishes from a little old lady.